The Novel Handbook

A complete guide to planning your novel
for plotters and pantsers alike

LAUREN CLARKE

Table of Contents

Introduction

Let me start by saying this: you are amazing. There are so many people in this world who want to write, who are forever thinking, "One day, I'll write this book." But life gets in the way.

You are not one of them. You know the secret: you have to make the time. You have to want this so badly you can taste it. And since time is such a precious commodity, you want to spend your writing time getting down words in as efficient a manner as possible.

That's why I've created *The Novel Handbook*. This book is designed to help you get moving on that project you're going to write by providing you with a work space where you can flesh out your story ideas. No, you don't need to be a plotter to use this book—this isn't just the big picture. It's about recording information on your characters—looks, loves, where they grew up, what makes them tick—and it's about keeping your timeline in check. It's about creating believable worlds and having a place you can look back to when you want to check on a fact, instead of searching through a Word document for the term "blue" in the hope of finding out what colour eyes your hero's sister has.

You're too amazing to waste time on things like that. You're a writer. You're going to get things done. So get that pen or pencil out, and put down the cup of coffee. It's time to shine.

Your Story

Title:...

Subtitle:..

Series: ....

Book number: ....

Genre: ....

Tip: *Don't forget to write the name of your project on the spine of this workbook so it's easy to select from your shelf.*

# Inspiration

What does this story mean to you?

··

··

··

··

··

··

··

··

··

··

··

··

Characters

Good characters are fundamental to any novel. They need to be detailed. They need to be three-dimensional, with flaws and strengths, beliefs and fears, just like real people. This is what will make them believable to your reader. This is what will change your novel from just a book into a story that resonates, with characters that aren't just characters, but book boyfriends, relatable heroines and understandable villains. This is what makes your novel memorable.

When it comes to your cast, the two leading characters (be they hero and heroine, hero and hero, or heroine and heroine) are some of the most important players in your novel. It is extremely important that you take care to learn everything about them, beyond just the physical.

Good leading characters complement each other. They build each other up, bringing out the best in each other, whether this is a romance or a friendship-based book.

Of course, in any good story, the two leading characters also have a source of tension. It's important to be thoroughly familiar with them so you know why they believe in what they do. Does your hero hate violence but your heroine is in an illegal underground ring, making it hard for them to forge a relationship? If so, why does the hero hate violence? Why does the heroine feel the need to fight?

Knowledge is power. The more you know about your characters, the better.

Hero 1

Name:..

Sex: ....

Age: .... **D.O.B.:** ....

Home town: ....

Occupation: ....

Study/training:..

Marital status: .... **Children:** ....

Hair colour:..

Hairstyle *(length etc)*:...

Eye colour (and does it ever change?):.................

....

Ethnicity:...

Body type:...

....

Skills — and how will these skills help your character in this story?

....

....

....

....

Flaws — and how will these flaws shape your character's role in this story?

....

....

....

....

Goal — what does your character want?

....

....

....

....

....

Motivation — why do they want this?

....

....

....

....

....

Conflict — what's getting in their way?

....

....

....

....

....

Do these goals change throughout the story, and if so, how?

....

....

....

....

....

....

....

....

....

How does this character relax?

....

....

What is his or her drink of choice (e.g. tea, coffee, alcohol, soda)?

....

....

What is his or her preferred snack?

....

....

Does he or she have any allergies?

....

....

Does he or she have any unique character tics (e.g. Does he always grind his jaw, or run a hand through his hair when stressed)?

....

....

....

....

When was his or her first kiss?

....

....

....

....

How does he or she relate to his or her family? Are they close?

....

....

Who is his or her closest friend?

....

....

People would describe him or her as:

....

....

....

....

The worst thing that could happen to him or her would be:

....

....

....

Should this happen in your story?

Hero 2

Name:..

Sex: ....

Age: .... **D.O.B.:** ....

Home town: ....

Occupation: ....

Study/training:..

Marital status: .... **Children:** ....

Hair colour:...

Hairstyle *(length etc)*:..

Eye colour (and does it ever change?):.................

....

Ethnicity:..

Body type:..

....

Skills — and how will these skills help your character in this story?

....

....

....

....

Flaws — and how will these flaws shape your character's role in this story?

....

....

....

....

Goal — what does your character want?

....

....

....

....

....

Motivation — why do they want this?

....

....

....

....

....

Conflict — what's getting in their way?

....

....

....

....

....

Do these goals change throughout the story, and if so, how?

··

··

··

··

··

··

··

··

··

How does this character relax?

··

··

What is his or her drink of choice (e.g. tea, coffee, alcohol, soda)?

··

··

What is his or her preferred snack?

....

....

Does he or she have any allergies?

....

....

**Does he or she have any unique character tics
(e.g. Does he always grind his jaw, or run a hand
through his hair when stressed)?**

....

....

....

....

When was his or her first kiss?

....

....

....

....

How does he or she relate to his or her family? Are they close?

....

....

Who is his or her closest friend?

....

....

People would describe him or her as:

....

....

....

....

The worst thing that could happen to him or her would be:

....

....

....

....

Should this happen in your story?

Villains

Our villains are often the chief source of conflict in our novels. When it comes to crafting a villain, it is important to make them a real person. Often, it can be easy to paint a villain as a truly evil psychopath, and while they do exist, a person of conflict will feel more real, more believable and therefore, scarier, if you keep them three-dimensional.

When writing your villain, make sure he or she:

- is smart, smart enough to be a worthy adversary to your heroes
- is occasionally kind, if not to your heroes then to someone else
- has a motivation for his or her actions that is stronger than just creating destruction
- has strengths that are a direct threat to your heroes
- is convinced that he or she is the hero of the novel

If you were to rewrite the story from the villain's POV, he or she should be able to be the hero. If you can do this, it's proof that you have created a villain who is strong and believable — and they can make the scariest bad guys of all.

"Every villain is a hero in his own mind"

Tom Hiddleston

Villain 1

Name:..

Sex: ....

Age: ....   **D.O.B.:** ....

Home town:...

Occupation: ....

Study/training:...

Marital status: .... **Children:** ....

Hair colour:...

Hairstyle (*length etc*):.......................................

Eye colour (and does it ever change?):................

....

Ethnicity:...

Body type:...

....

Skills—and how will these skills help your character in this story?

....

....

....

....

Flaws—and how will these flaws shape your character's role in this story?

....

....

....

....

Goal—what does your character want?

....

....

....

....

....

Motivation—why do they want this?

....

....

....

....

....

Conflict—what's getting in their way?

....

....

....

....

Do these goals change throughout the story, and if so, how?

....

....

....

....

....

....

....

....

....

How does this character relax?

....

....

What is his or her drink of choice (e.g. tea, coffee, alcohol, soda)?

....

....

What is his or her preferred snack?

....

....

Does he or she have any allergies?

....

....

Does he or she have any unique character tics (e.g. Does he always grind his jaw, or run a hand through his hair when stressed)?

....

....

....

....

When was his or her first kiss?

....

....

....

....

How does he or she relate to his or her family? Are they close?

....

....

Who is his or her closest friend?

....

....

People would describe him or her as:

....

....

....

....

The worst thing that could happen to him or her would be:

....

....

....

....

Should this happen in your story?

Villain 2

Name:..

Sex: ....

Age: ....   **D.O.B.:** ....

Home town:..

Occupation: ....

Study/training:..

Marital status: ....   **Children:** ....

Hair colour:...

Hairstyle *(length etc)*:......................................

Eye colour (and does it ever change?):................

....

Ethnicity:..

Body type:..

....

Skills—and how will these skills help your character in this story?

....

....

....

....

Flaws—and how will these flaws shape your character's role in this story?

....

....

....

....

Goal—what does your character want?

....

....

....

....

Motivation—why do they want this?

....

....

....

....

Conflict—what's getting in their way?

....

....

....

....

Do these goals change throughout the story, and if so, how?

....

....

....

....

....

....

....

....

....

How does this character relax?

....

....

What is his or her drink of choice (e.g. tea, coffee, alcohol, soda)?

....

....

What is his or her preferred snack?

....

....

Does he or she have any allergies?

....

....

Does he or she have any unique character tics (e.g. Does he always grind his jaw, or run a hand through his hair when stressed)?

....

....

....

....

When was his or her first kiss?

....

....

....

....

How does he or she relate to his or her family? Are they close?

....

....

Who is his or her closest friend?

....

....

People would describe him or her as:

....

....

....

....

The worst thing that could happen to him or her would be:

....

....

....

....

Should this happen in your story?

Supporting Characters

Having a strong cast of supporting characters is crucial to your story. Just like when creating our villain, we need to try and avoid cliché (e.g. the ditzy and popular best female friend, the muscle man who's all brawn and no brain).

As with our leading members of cast, the minor characters should have attributes that make them more than just bodies to flesh out a scene (e.g. "I need someone for my hero to talk to when he's trying to figure out the villain's motivation."). Your cast of supporting characters is better than that.

Fill out the questions in the pages that follow and remember to ask yourself if you can cut any of these characters out by assigning their role to another character. Make sure every person on your page is strong and there for a reason—the story is stronger for their presence.

# *Character 1*

Name: ....

Sex: ....

Age: .... **D.O.B.:** ....

Home town: ....

Occupation: ....

Study/training: ....

Marital status: .... **Children:** ....

Hair colour: ....

Hairstyle *(length etc)*: ....

Eye colour (and does it ever change?): ....

....

Ethnicity:...

Body type:..

....

Skills:...

....

....

....

Flaws:...

....

....

Role in your story:..

....

....

....

Can this role be completed by another character?

YES ☐   **NO** ☐

Character 2

Name: ....

Sex: ....

Age: .... **D.O.B.:** ....

Home town: ....

Occupation: ....

Study/training: ....

Marital status: .... **Children:** ....

Hair colour: ....

Hairstyle *(length etc)*: ....

Eye colour (and does it ever change?): ....
....

Ethnicity:..

Body type:...

....

Skills:...

....

....

....

Flaws:..

....

....

Role in your story:..

....

....

....

Can this role be completed by another character?

YES ☐   NO ☐

Character 3

Name: ....

Sex: ....

Age: .... D.O.B.: ....

Home town: ....

Occupation: ....

Study/training: ....

Marital status: .... Children: ....

Hair colour: ....

Hairstyle *(length etc)*: ....

Eye colour (and does it ever change?):...............
....

Ethnicity:...

Body type:...

....

Skills:..

....

....

....

Flaws:..

....

....

....

Role in your story:...

....

....

....

Can this role be completed by another character?

YES ☐   NO ☐

Character 4

Name: ....

Sex: ....

Age: .... **D.O.B.:** ....

Home town: ....

Occupation: ....

Study/training: ....

Marital status: .... **Children:** ....

Hair colour: ....

Hairstyle *(length etc)*: ....

Eye colour (and does it ever change?): ....

....

Ethnicity:..

Body type:..

....

Skills:..

....

....

....

Flaws:..

....

....

....

Role in your story:......................................

....

....

....

Can this role be completed by another character?

YES ☐   NO ☐

Character 5

Name: ....

Sex:...

Age:.............................. **D.O.B.:** ....

Home town:...

Occupation: ....

Study/training: ....

Marital status: .... **Children:** ....

Hair colour: ....

Hairstyle *(length etc):* ....

Eye colour (and does it ever change?):.................

....

Ethnicity:...

Body type:...

....

Skills:...

....

....

....

Flaws:...

....

....

Role in your story:...

....

....

....

Can this role be completed by another character?

YES ☐   **NO** ☐

Character 6

Name: ....

Sex: ....

Age: .... **D.O.B.:** ....

Home town: ....

Occupation: ....

Study/training: ....

Marital status: .... **Children:** ....

Hair colour: ....

Hairstyle (*length etc*): ....

Eye colour (and does it ever change?): ....

....

Ethnicity:...

Body type:..

....

Skills:..

....

....

....

Flaws:...

....

....

....

Role in your story:..

....

....

....

Can this role be completed by another character?

YES ☐   NO ☐

Character 7

Name: ....

Sex: ....

Age: .... **D.O.B.:** ....

Home town: ....

Occupation: ....

Study/training: ....

Marital status: .... **Children:** ....

Hair colour: ....

Hairstyle *(length etc)*: ....

Eye colour (and does it ever change?): ....

....

Ethnicity:...

Body type:...

....

Skills:...

....

....

Flaws:...

....

....

Role in your story:...

....

....

Can this role be completed by another character?

YES ☐   **NO** ☐

Character 8

Name: ....

Sex: ....

Age: .... **D.O.B.:** ....

Home town: ....

Occupation: ....

Study/training: ....

Marital status: .... **Children:** ....

Hair colour: ....

Hairstyle *(length etc)***:** ....

Eye colour (and does it ever change?): ....
....

Ethnicity:...

Body type:...

....

Skills:...

....

....

....

Flaws:...

....

....

Role in your story:..

....

....

Can this role be completed by another character?

YES ☐   NO ☐

Character 9

Name: ....

Sex:..

Age:................................ D.O.B.: ....

Home town:..

Occupation: ....

Study/training: ....

Marital status: .... Children: ....

Hair colour: ....

Hairstyle *(length etc)*: ....

Eye colour (and does it ever change?):................

....

Ethnicity:..

Body type:...

....

Skills:..

....

....

....

Flaws:..

....

....

....

Role in your story:...

....

....

....

Can this role be completed by another character?

YES ☐   NO ☐

Character 10

Name: ....

Sex: ....

Age: .... **D.O.B.:** ....

Home town: ....

Occupation: ....

Study/training: ....

Marital status: .... **Children:** ....

Hair colour: ....

Hairstyle *(length etc)*: ....

Eye colour (and does it ever change?): ....

....

Ethnicity:..

Body type:...

....

Skills:..

....

....

....

Flaws:..

....

....

Role in your story:..

....

....

....

Can this role be completed by another
character?

YES [ ]   NO [ ]

Character 11

Name: ....

Sex: ....

Age: .... D.O.B.: ....

Home town: ....

Occupation: ....

Study/training: ....

Marital status: .... Children: ....

Hair colour: ....

Hairstyle *(length etc)*: ....

Eye colour (and does it ever change?): ....

....

Ethnicity:..

Body type:...

....

Skills:..

....

....

....

Flaws:..

....

....

....

Role in your story:...

....

....

....

Can this role be completed by another character?

YES ☐   NO ☐

Character 12

Name: ....

Sex: ....

Age: .... **D.O.B.:** ....

Home town: ....

Occupation: ....

Study/training: ....

Marital status: .... **Children:** ....

Hair colour: ....

Hairstyle *(length etc)*: ....

Eye colour (and does it ever change?): ....

....

Ethnicity:...

Body type:...

....

Skills:..

....

....

....

Flaws:...

....

....

....

Role in your story:..

....

....

....

Can this role be completed by another character?

YES ☐   NO ☐

Character 13

Name: ....

Sex: ....

Age: .... D.O.B.: ....

Home town: ....

Occupation: ....

Study/training: ....

Marital status: .... Children: ....

Hair colour: ....

Hairstyle *(length etc)*: ....

Eye colour (and does it ever change?): ....
....

Ethnicity:...

Body type:...

....

Skills:...

....

....

....

Flaws:..

....

....

....

Role in your story:...

....

....

....

Can this role be completed by another character?

YES ☐   NO ☐

Character 14

Name: ....

Sex: ....

Age: .... **D.O.B.:** ....

Home town: ....

Occupation: ....

Study/training: ....

Marital status: .... **Children:** ....

Hair colour: ....

Hairstyle *(length etc)*: ....

Eye colour (and does it ever change?): ....

....

Ethnicity:..

Body type:...

....

Skills:...

....

....

....

Flaws:...

....

....

....

Role in your story:...

....

....

....

Can this role be completed by another character?

YES ☐   NO ☐

Character 15

Name: ....

Sex: ....

Age: .... **D.O.B.:** ....

Home town: ....

Occupation: ....

Study/training: ....

Marital status: .... **Children:** ....

Hair colour: ....

Hairstyle *(length etc)*: ....

Eye colour (and does it ever change?): ....

....

Ethnicity:..

Body type:...

....

Skills:..

....

....

....

Flaws:...

....

....

....

Role in your story:..

....

....

....

Can this role be completed by another character?

YES ☐   NO ☐

Character 16

Name: ....

Sex: ....

Age: .... **D.O.B.:** ....

Home town: ....

Occupation: ....

Study/training: ....

Marital status: .... **Children:** ....

Hair colour: ....

Hairstyle *(length etc)***:** ....

Eye colour (and does it ever change?): ....

....

Ethnicity:..

Body type:...

....

Skills:..

....

....

....

Flaws:...

....

....

....

Role in your story:...

....

....

....

Can this role be completed by another character?

YES ☐   NO ☐

Character 17

Name: ....

Sex: ....

Age: ....   **D.O.B.:** ....

Home town: ....

Occupation: ....

Study/training: ....

Marital status: ....   **Children:** ....

Hair colour: ....

Hairstyle *(length etc)***:** ....

Eye colour (and does it ever change?): ....

....

Ethnicity:..

Body type:...

....

Skills:...

....

....

....

Flaws:...

....

....

Role in your story:..

....

....

Can this role be completed by another character?

YES ☐   NO ☐

Character 18

Name: ....

Sex: ....

Age: .... **D.O.B.:** ....

Home town: ....

Occupation: ....

Study/training: ....

Marital status: .... **Children:** ....

Hair colour: ....

Hairstyle (*length etc*): ....

Eye colour (and does it ever change?): ....
....

Ethnicity:...

Body type:...

....

Skills:..

....

....

....

Flaws:..

....

....

....

Role in your story:...

....

....

....

Can this role be completed by another character?

YES ☐   NO ☐

Character 19

Name: ....

Sex: ....

Age: .... **D.O.B.:** ....

Home town: ....

Occupation: ....

Study/training: ....

Marital status: .... **Children:** ....

Hair colour: ....

Hairstyle (*length etc*): ....

Eye colour (and does it ever change?): ....
....

Ethnicity:..

Body type:...

....

Skills:...

....

....

....

Flaws:..

....

....

....

Role in your story:..

....

....

....

Can this role be completed by another character?

YES ☐   NO ☐

Character 20

Name: ....

Sex: ....

Age: .... **D.O.B.:** ....

Home town: ....

Occupation: ....

Study/training: ....

Marital status: .... **Children:** ....

Hair colour: ....

Hairstyle (*length etc*): ....

Eye colour (and does it ever change?): ....

....

Ethnicity:...

Body type:...

....

Skills:...

....

....

....

Flaws:...

....

....

Role in your story:...

....

....

Can this role be completed by another character?

YES ☐   NO ☐

# World

Setting is an important part of your story. Where is your story set? Think about the town, your hero's house, the place where your major conflict (black moment) will take place. Is this the best location for this part of your story? What locations will you need to use in your story and what features will distinguish them?

LOCATION ONE

Description:...

....

....

....

....

....

LOCATION TWO

Description: ....
....
....
....
....

LOCATION THREE

Description: ....
....
....
....
....

LOCATION FOUR

Description: ....
....
....
....

LOCATION FIVE

Description:..

....

....

....

....

LOCATION SIX

Description:..

....

....

....

....

LOCATION SEVEN

Description:..

....

....

....

LOCATION EIGHT

Description: ....
....
....
....
....

LOCATION NINE

Description: ....
....
....
....
....

LOCATION TEN

Description: ....
....
....
....
....

World (cont.)

On a broader scale, what world is this set in? What are the political and religious beliefs of your characters, and are they the same as the views of the society? What laws do your characters abide by?

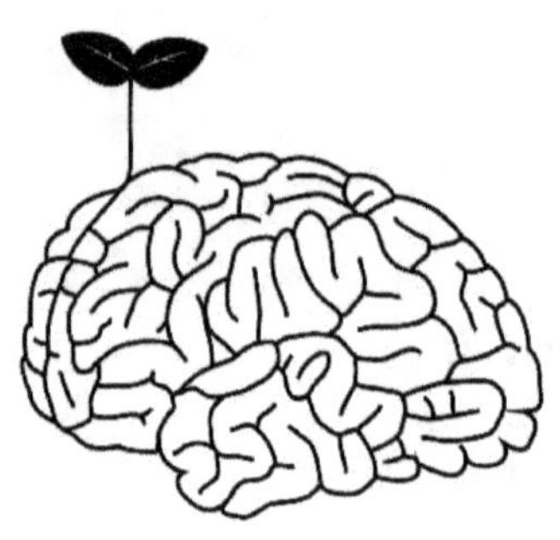

"*Research is creating new knowledge.*"

Neil Armstrong

Research

Research can make the difference between a good story and a great one. Whether it's investigating how to make the perfect cup of coffee or how to hide a dead body, you can never do too much research. It's the little things, those small details that show you know what your characters are going through, that can make all the difference in a book.

Use these pages to make notes on the research you need for this manuscript. When possible, try to engage in any activity yourself to try and get a true perspective and allow for greater truth in your work (illegal activity not encouraged).

Chapter Tracking

Keeping track of the action in your story can require a little work. Use the following pages to create a summary of the action that occurs in each chapter of your book.

Tip: *This can be a good tool to use when revising.*

PROLOGUE: ....

....

....

ONE: ....

....

....

TWO: ....

....

....

....

THREE: ....

....

....

....

FOUR: ....

....

....

....

FIVE: ....

....

TWO: ....

....

SIX: ....

....

....

....

SEVEN: ....

....

....

....

EIGHT: ....

....

....

....

NINE: ....

....

....

....

TEN: ....

....

....

....

ELEVEN: ....

....

....

....

TWELVE: ....

....

....

....

THIRTEEN: ....

....

....

....

FOURTEEN: ....

....

....

....

FIFTEEN: ....

....

....

....

SIXTEEN: ....

....

....

....

SEVENTEEN: ....

....

....

EIGHTEEN: ....

....

....

....

NINETEEN: ....

....

....

....

TWENTY: ....

....

....

....

TWENTY-ONE: ....

....

....

TWENTY-TWO: ....

....

....

....

TWENTY-THREE: ....

....

....

....

TWENTY-FOUR: ....

....

....

....

TWENTY-FIVE: ....

....

....

....

TWENTY-SIX: ....

....

....

....

TWENTY-SEVEN: ....

....

....

....

TWENTY-EIGHT: ....

....

....

....

TWENTY-NINE: ....

....

....

....

THIRTY: ....

....

....

....

THIRTY-ONE: ....

....

....

....

THIRTY-TWO: ....

....

....

....

THIRTY-THREE: ....

....

....

....

THIRTY-FOUR: ....

....

....

....

THIRTY-FIVE: ....

....

....

....

THIRTY-SIX: ....

....

....

THIRTY-SEVEN: ....

....

....

THIRTY-EIGHT: ....

....

....

....

THIRTY-NINE: ....

....

....

....

FORTY: ....

....

....

....

FORTY-ONE: ....

....

....

....

FORTY-TWO: ....

....

....

....

FORTY-THREE: ....

....

....

....

FORTY-FOUR: ....

....

....

....

FORTY-FIVE: ....

....

....

....

FORTY-SIX: ....

....

....

....

FORTY-SEVEN: ....

....

....

FORTY-EIGHT: ....

....

....

FORTY-NINE: ....

....

....

FIFTY: ....

....

....

....

EPILOGUE: ....

....

....

Tip: *Remember to ask yourself:*
Is this moving the story forward?

Loose Ends

It happens to the best of us — we're mid-sprint or revising, and we see something that makes us think "Ah, I'll flesh that out later."

Or, perhaps it works in reverse. You're in the final stages of the book, and your hero is confronting your villain with the knife you ingeniously planted in the scene seven chapters earlier — only, you haven't actually done that yet.

Make a note of all your loose ends here and then come back later to check they're all resolved.

Loose End	Tied

Loose End	Tied

Language

The language you use is an essential part of every book. Sometimes, you may use terms that aren't everyday parts of your vernacular (thanks to your stellar research into your hero's occupation, for example), or perhaps you have a character who speaks a foreign language. Maybe it's simpler than that. Perhaps you've just got a character with a surname that your fingers trip over every time you try to type it!

Place all those strange words and phrases over the next few pages along with a brief description so you have a good reference point when continuing your writing.

Term: ....

Relevance: ....

....

....

Term:..

Relevance: ....

....

....

Term:..

Relevance: ....

....

....

Term:..

Relevance: ....

....

....

Term:..

Relevance: ....

....

....

Term: ....

Relevance: ....

....

....

Term: ....

Relevance: ....

....

....

Term: ....

Relevance: ....

....

....

Term: ....

Relevance: ....

....

....

Timeline

Timeline is one of the most common things that can get convoluted or go wrong in a story. One easy solution? Plot out the events that happen in your story using the calendars on the pages that follow. Simply put the dates in the top corners of the boxes (depending on what year your story takes place in). Consider the days of the week, when your story takes place, and if there are any public holidays or national events that should be observed during the period your story is set in.

Tip: *Even on days when your character isn't engaging in action on the page, you can make mention of what they're doing using this tracker, so you know where they are.*

MONTH:

Mon	Tues	Wed	Thurs	Fri	Sat	Sun

MONTH:

Mon	Tues	Wed	Thurs	Fri	Sat	Sun

MONTH:

Mon	Tues	Wed	Thurs	Fri	Sat	Sun

MONTH:

Mon	Tues	Wed	Thurs	Fri	Sat	Sun

MONTH:

Mon	Tues	Wed	Thurs	Fri	Sat	Sun

# Goals

You've got this. Let's get it done!

X	Deadline	Goal

X	Deadline	Goal

X	Deadline	Goal

X	Deadline	Goal

Project Tracker

Writing a novel shouldn't just be about setting goals and meeting them—it should be about celebrating the amazing things you've done! Write your weekly goals below and then detail what you've done to help achieve them on a daily basis. It's not all words on a page—sometimes it's about letting ideas develop in our minds.

WEEKLY GOAL: *(this can be word count, editing-related, planning … the sky's the limit)*

Monday: *What have you achieved on this date?*

Tuesday: ....

Wednesday: ....

Thursday: ....

Friday: ....

Saturday: ....

Sunday: ....

WEEKLY GOAL:..

....

Monday: ....

Tuesday: ....

Wednesday: ....

Thursday: ....

Friday: ....

Saturday: ....

Sunday: ....

WEEKLY GOAL:..

....

Monday: ....

Tuesday: ....

Wednesday: ....

Thursday: ....

Friday: ....

Saturday: ....

Sunday: ....

WEEKLY GOAL: ....

....

Monday: ....

Tuesday: ....

Wednesday: ....

Thursday: ....

Friday: ....

Saturday: ....

Sunday: ....

WEEKLY GOAL: ....

....

Monday: ....

Tuesday: ....

Wednesday: ....

Thursday: ....

Friday: ....

Saturday: ....

Sunday: ....

WEEKLY GOAL:...

....

Monday: ....

Tuesday: ....

Wednesday: ....

Thursday: ....

Friday: ....

Saturday: ....

Sunday: ....

WEEKLY GOAL:...

....

Monday: ....

Tuesday: ....

Wednesday: ....

Thursday: ....

Friday: ....

Saturday: ....

Sunday: ....

WEEKLY GOAL: ....

....

Monday: ....

Tuesday: ....

Wednesday: ....

Thursday: ....

Friday: ....

Saturday: ....

Sunday: ....

WEEKLY GOAL: ....

....

Monday: ....

Tuesday: ....

Wednesday: ....

Thursday: ....

Friday: ....

Saturday: ....

Sunday: ....

WEEKLY GOAL:..

....

Monday: ....

Tuesday: ....

Wednesday: ....

Thursday: ....

Friday: ....

Saturday: ....

Sunday: ....

WEEKLY GOAL:..

....

Monday: ....

Tuesday: ....

Wednesday: ....

Thursday: ....

Friday: ....

Saturday: ....

Sunday: ....

WEEKLY GOAL: ....

....

Monday: ....

Tuesday: ....

Wednesday: ....

Thursday: ....

Friday: ....

Saturday: ....

Sunday: ....

WEEKLY GOAL: ....

....

Monday: ....

Tuesday: ....

Wednesday: ....

Thursday: ....

Friday: ....

Saturday: ....

Sunday: ....

WEEKLY GOAL:...

....

Monday: ....

Tuesday: ....

Wednesday: ....

Thursday: ....

Friday: ....

Saturday: ....

Sunday: ....

WEEKLY GOAL:...

....

Monday: ....

Tuesday: ....

Wednesday: ....

Thursday: ....

Friday: ....

Saturday: ....

Sunday: ....

WEEKLY GOAL: ....

....

Monday: ....

Tuesday: ....

Wednesday: ....

Thursday: ....

Friday: ....

Saturday: ....

Sunday: ....

WEEKLY GOAL: ....

....

Monday: ....

Tuesday: ....

Wednesday: ....

Thursday: ....

Friday: ....

Saturday: ....

Sunday: ....

WEEKLY GOAL:...

....

Monday: ....

Tuesday: ....

Wednesday: ....

Thursday: ....

Friday: ....

Saturday: ....

Sunday: ....

WEEKLY GOAL:...

....

Monday: ....

Tuesday: ....

Wednesday: ....

Thursday: ....

Friday: ....

Saturday: ....

Sunday: ....

WEEKLY GOAL:...

....

Monday: ....

Tuesday: ....

Wednesday: ....

Thursday: ....

Friday: ....

Saturday: ....

Sunday: ....

WEEKLY GOAL:...

....

Monday: ....

Tuesday: ....

Wednesday: ....

Thursday: ....

Friday: ....

Saturday: ....

Sunday: ....

WEEKLY GOAL:...

....

Monday: ....

Tuesday: ....

Wednesday: ....

Thursday: ....

Friday: ....

Saturday: ....

Sunday: ....

WEEKLY GOAL:...

....

Monday: ....

Tuesday: ....

Wednesday: ....

Thursday: ....

Friday: ....

Saturday: ....

Sunday: ....

WEEKLY GOAL: ....

....

Monday: ....

Tuesday: ....

Wednesday: ....

Thursday: ....

Friday: ....

Saturday: ....

Sunday: ....

WEEKLY GOAL: ....

....

Monday: ....

Tuesday: ....

Wednesday: ....

Thursday: ....

Friday: ....

Saturday: ....

Sunday: ....

WEEKLY GOAL:...

....

Monday: ....

Tuesday: ....

Wednesday: ....

Thursday: ....

Friday: ....

Saturday: ....

Sunday: ....

WEEKLY GOAL:...

....

Monday: ....

Tuesday: ....

Wednesday: ....

Thursday: ....

Friday: ....

Saturday: ....

Sunday: ....

WEEKLY GOAL: ....

....

Monday: ....

Tuesday: ....

Wednesday: ....

Thursday: ....

Friday: ....

Saturday: ....

Sunday: ....

WEEKLY GOAL: ....

....

Monday: ....

Tuesday: ....

Wednesday: ....

Thursday: ....

Friday: ....

Saturday: ....

Sunday: ....

WEEKLY GOAL:..

....

Monday: ....

Tuesday: ....

Wednesday: ....

Thursday: ....

Friday: ....

Saturday: ....

Sunday: ....

WEEKLY GOAL:..

....

Monday: ....

Tuesday: ....

Wednesday: ....

Thursday: ....

Friday: ....

Saturday: ....

Sunday: ....

Dream Team

It takes a village, right? Who is on your team when it comes to completing your novel?

Beta readers:..

....

....

....

Date booked for:...

Editors:..

....

Date booked for:...

Cover designer: ....

Date booked for:...

Formatter: ....

Date booked for:..

PR or marketing: ....

....

....

....

Date booked for:..

Reviewers will help your book gain traction and help word-of-mouth spread about your masterpiece.

Reviewer name	Date contacted	Response

Reviewer name	Date contacted	Response

Pre-edit Check-list

Congratulations! You've done it. You've finally finished your novel, it's been to a beta or two, and now you're ready to hand it to the editor.

But before you do, here are a few things you should check in each chapter:

PROLOGUE:

Are the characters described (their current action, appearance, emotions)? YES ☐ NO ☐

Are more senses than just sight utilised (e.g. taste, smell)? YES ☐ NO ☐

Does the plot progress? YES ☐ NO ☐

Are all necessary characters in this chapter? YES ☐ NO ☐

Is there conflict? YES ☐ NO ☐

Are the consequences of this chapter followed up? YES ☐ NO ☐

CHAPTER ONE:

Are the characters described (their current action, appearance, emotions)? YES ☐ NO ☐

Are more senses than just sight utilised (e.g. taste, smell)? YES ☐ NO ☐

Does the plot progress? YES ☐ NO ☐

Are all necessary characters in this chapter? YES ☐ NO ☐

Is there conflict? YES ☐ NO ☐

Are the consequences of this chapter followed up? YES ☐ NO ☐

CHAPTER TWO:

Are the characters described (their current action, appearance, emotions)?	YES ☐	NO ☐
Are more senses than just sight utilised (e.g. taste, smell)?	YES ☐	NO ☐
Does the plot progress?	YES ☐	NO ☐
Are all necessary characters in this chapter?	YES ☐	NO ☐
Is there conflict?	YES ☐	NO ☐
Are the consequences of this chapter followed up?	YES ☐	NO ☐

CHAPTER THREE:

Are the characters described (their current action, appearance, emotions)?	YES ☐	NO ☐
Are more senses than just sight utilised (e.g. taste, smell)?	YES ☐	NO ☐
Does the plot progress?	YES ☐	NO ☐
Are all necessary characters in this chapter?	YES ☐	NO ☐
Is there conflict?	YES ☐	NO ☐
Are the consequences of this chapter followed up?	YES ☐	NO ☐

CHAPTER FOUR:

Are the characters described (their current action, appearance, emotions)?	YES ☐	NO ☐
Are more senses than just sight utilised (e.g. taste, smell)?	YES ☐	NO ☐
Does the plot progress?	YES ☐	NO ☐
Are all necessary characters in this chapter?	YES ☐	NO ☐
Is there conflict?	YES ☐	NO ☐
Are the consequences of this chapter followed up?	YES ☐	NO ☐

CHAPTER FIVE:

Are the characters described (their current action, appearance, emotions)?	YES ☐	NO ☐
Are more senses than just sight utilised (e.g. taste, smell)?	YES ☐	NO ☐
Does the plot progress?	YES ☐	NO ☐
Are all necessary characters in this chapter?	YES ☐	NO ☐
Is there conflict?	YES ☐	NO ☐
Are the consequences of this chapter followed up?	YES ☐	NO ☐

CHAPTER SIX:

Are the characters described (their current action, appearance, emotions)?	YES ☐	NO ☐
Are more senses than just sight utilised (e.g. taste, smell)?	YES ☐	NO ☐
Does the plot progress?	YES ☐	NO ☐
Are all necessary characters in this chapter?	YES ☐	NO ☐
Is there conflict?	YES ☐	NO ☐
Are the consequences of this chapter followed up?	YES ☐	NO ☐

CHAPTER SEVEN:

Are the characters described (their current action, appearance, emotions)?	YES ☐	NO ☐
Are more senses than just sight utilised (e.g. taste, smell)?	YES ☐	NO ☐
Does the plot progress?	YES ☐	NO ☐
Are all necessary characters in this chapter?	YES ☐	NO ☐
Is there conflict?	YES ☐	NO ☐
Are the consequences of this chapter followed up?	YES ☐	NO ☐

CHAPTER EIGHT:

Are the characters described (their current action, appearance, emotions)?	YES ☐	NO ☐
Are more senses than just sight utilised (e.g. taste, smell)?	YES ☐	NO ☐
Does the plot progress?	YES ☐	NO ☐
Are all necessary characters in this chapter?	YES ☐	NO ☐
Is there conflict?	YES ☐	NO ☐
Are the consequences of this chapter followed up?	YES ☐	NO ☐

CHAPTER NINE:

Are the characters described (their current action, appearance, emotions)?	YES ☐	NO ☐
Are more senses than just sight utilised (e.g. taste, smell)?	YES ☐	NO ☐
Does the plot progress?	YES ☐	NO ☐
Are all necessary characters in this chapter?	YES ☐	NO ☐
Is there conflict?	YES ☐	NO ☐
Are the consequences of this chapter followed up?	YES ☐	NO ☐

CHAPTER TEN:

Are the characters described (their current action, appearance, emotions)?	YES ☐	NO ☐
Are more senses than just sight utilised (e.g. taste, smell)?	YES ☐	NO ☐
Does the plot progress?	YES ☐	NO ☐
Are all necessary characters in this chapter?	YES ☐	NO ☐
Is there conflict?	YES ☐	NO ☐
Are the consequences of this chapter followed up?	YES ☐	NO ☐

CHAPTER ELEVEN:

Are the characters described (their current action, appearance, emotions)?	YES ☐	NO ☐
Are more senses than just sight utilised (e.g. taste, smell)?	YES ☐	NO ☐
Does the plot progress?	YES ☐	NO ☐
Are all necessary characters in this chapter?	YES ☐	NO ☐
Is there conflict?	YES ☐	NO ☐
Are the consequences of this chapter followed up?	YES ☐	NO ☐

CHAPTER TWELVE:

Are the characters described (their current action, appearance, emotions)?	YES ☐	NO ☐
Are more senses than just sight utilised (e.g. taste, smell)?	YES ☐	NO ☐
Does the plot progress?	YES ☐	NO ☐
Are all necessary characters in this chapter?	YES ☐	NO ☐
Is there conflict?	YES ☐	NO ☐
Are the consequences of this chapter followed up?	YES ☐	NO ☐

CHAPTER THIRTEEN:

Are the characters described (their current action, appearance, emotions)?	YES ☐	NO ☐
Are more senses than just sight utilised (e.g. taste, smell)?	YES ☐	NO ☐
Does the plot progress?	YES ☐	NO ☐
Are all necessary characters in this chapter?	YES ☐	NO ☐
Is there conflict?	YES ☐	NO ☐
Are the consequences of this chapter followed up?	YES ☐	NO ☐

CHAPTER FOURTEEN:

Are the characters described (their current action, appearance, emotions)?	YES ☐	NO ☐
Are more senses than just sight utilised (e.g. taste, smell)?	YES ☐	NO ☐
Does the plot progress?	YES ☐	NO ☐
Are all necessary characters in this chapter?	YES ☐	NO ☐
Is there conflict?	YES ☐	NO ☐
Are the consequences of this chapter followed up?	YES ☐	NO ☐

CHAPTER FIFTEEN:

Are the characters described (their current action, appearance, emotions)?	YES ☐	NO ☐
Are more senses than just sight utilised (e.g. taste, smell)?	YES ☐	NO ☐
Does the plot progress?	YES ☐	NO ☐
Are all necessary characters in this chapter?	YES ☐	NO ☐
Is there conflict?	YES ☐	NO ☐
Are the consequences of this chapter followed up?	YES ☐	NO ☐

CHAPTER SIXTEEN:

Are the characters described (their current action, appearance, emotions)?	YES ☐	NO ☐
Are more senses than just sight utilised (e.g. taste, smell)?	YES ☐	NO ☐
Does the plot progress?	YES ☐	NO ☐
Are all necessary characters in this chapter?	YES ☐	NO ☐
Is there conflict?	YES ☐	NO ☐
Are the consequences of this chapter followed up?	YES ☐	NO ☐

CHAPTER SEVENTEEN:

Are the characters described (their current action, appearance, emotions)?	YES ☐	NO ☐
Are more senses than just sight utilised (e.g. taste, smell)?	YES ☐	NO ☐
Does the plot progress?	YES ☐	NO ☐
Are all necessary characters in this chapter?	YES ☐	NO ☐
Is there conflict?	YES ☐	NO ☐
Are the consequences of this chapter followed up?	YES ☐	NO ☐

CHAPTER EIGHTEEN:

Are the characters described (their current action, appearance, emotions)?	YES ☐	NO ☐
Are more senses than just sight utilised (e.g. taste, smell)?	YES ☐	NO ☐
Does the plot progress?	YES ☐	NO ☐
Are all necessary characters in this chapter?	YES ☐	NO ☐
Is there conflict?	YES ☐	NO ☐
Are the consequences of this chapter followed up?	YES ☐	NO ☐

CHAPTER NINETEEN:

Are the characters described (their current action, appearance, emotions)?	YES ☐	NO ☐
Are more senses than just sight utilised (e.g. taste, smell)?	YES ☐	NO ☐
Does the plot progress?	YES ☐	NO ☐
Are all necessary characters in this chapter?	YES ☐	NO ☐
Is there conflict?	YES ☐	NO ☐
Are the consequences of this chapter followed up?	YES ☐	NO ☐

CHAPTER TWENTY:

Are the characters described (their current action, appearance, emotions)? — YES ☐ NO ☐

Are more senses than just sight utilised (e.g. taste, smell)? — YES ☐ NO ☐

Does the plot progress? — YES ☐ NO ☐

Are all necessary characters in this chapter? — YES ☐ NO ☐

Is there conflict? — YES ☐ NO ☐

Are the consequences of this chapter followed up? — YES ☐ NO ☐

CHAPTER TWENTY-ONE:

Are the characters described (their current action, appearance, emotions)? — YES ☐ NO ☐

Are more senses than just sight utilised (e.g. taste, smell)? — YES ☐ NO ☐

Does the plot progress? — YES ☐ NO ☐

Are all necessary characters in this chapter? — YES ☐ NO ☐

Is there conflict? — YES ☐ NO ☐

Are the consequences of this chapter followed up? — YES ☐ NO ☐

CHAPTER TWENTY-TWO:

Are the characters described (their current action, appearance, emotions)? — YES ☐ NO ☐

Are more senses than just sight utilised (e.g. taste, smell)? — YES ☐ NO ☐

Does the plot progress? — YES ☐ NO ☐

Are all necessary characters in this chapter? — YES ☐ NO ☐

Is there conflict? — YES ☐ NO ☐

Are the consequences of this chapter followed up? — YES ☐ NO ☐

CHAPTER TWENTY-THREE:

Are the characters described (their current action, appearance, emotions)?	YES ☐	NO ☐
Are more senses than just sight utilised (e.g. taste, smell)?	YES ☐	NO ☐
Does the plot progress?	YES ☐	NO ☐
Are all necessary characters in this chapter?	YES ☐	NO ☐
Is there conflict?	YES ☐	NO ☐
Are the consequences of this chapter followed up?	YES ☐	NO ☐

CHAPTER TWENTY-FOUR:

Are the characters described (their current action, appearance, emotions)?	YES ☐	NO ☐
Are more senses than just sight utilised (e.g. taste, smell)?	YES ☐	NO ☐
Does the plot progress?	YES ☐	NO ☐
Are all necessary characters in this chapter?	YES ☐	NO ☐
Is there conflict?	YES ☐	NO ☐
Are the consequences of this chapter followed up?	YES ☐	NO ☐

CHAPTER TWENTY-FIVE:

Are the characters described (their current action, appearance, emotions)?	YES ☐	NO ☐
Are more senses than just sight utilised (e.g. taste, smell)?	YES ☐	NO ☐
Does the plot progress?	YES ☐	NO ☐
Are all necessary characters in this chapter?	YES ☐	NO ☐
Is there conflict?	YES ☐	NO ☐
Are the consequences of this chapter followed up?	YES ☐	NO ☐

CHAPTER TWENTY-SIX:

Are the characters described (their current action, appearance, emotions)?	YES ☐	NO ☐
Are more senses than just sight utilised (e.g. taste, smell)?	YES ☐	NO ☐
Does the plot progress?	YES ☐	NO ☐
Are all necessary characters in this chapter?	YES ☐	NO ☐
Is there conflict?	YES ☐	NO ☐
Are the consequences of this chapter followed up?	YES ☐	NO ☐

CHAPTER TWENTY-SEVEN:

Are the characters described (their current action, appearance, emotions)?	YES ☐	NO ☐
Are more senses than just sight utilised (e.g. taste, smell)?	YES ☐	NO ☐
Does the plot progress?	YES ☐	NO ☐
Are all necessary characters in this chapter?	YES ☐	NO ☐
Is there conflict?	YES ☐	NO ☐
Are the consequences of this chapter followed up?	YES ☐	NO ☐

CHAPTER TWENTY-EIGHT:

Are the characters described (their current action, appearance, emotions)?	YES ☐	NO ☐
Are more senses than just sight utilised (e.g. taste, smell)?	YES ☐	NO ☐
Does the plot progress?	YES ☐	NO ☐
Are all necessary characters in this chapter?	YES ☐	NO ☐
Is there conflict?	YES ☐	NO ☐
Are the consequences of this chapter followed up?	YES ☐	NO ☐

CHAPTER TWENTY-NINE:

Are the characters described (their current action, appearance, emotions)?	YES ☐	NO ☐
Are more senses than just sight utilised (e.g. taste, smell)?	YES ☐	NO ☐
Does the plot progress?	YES ☐	NO ☐
Are all necessary characters in this chapter?	YES ☐	NO ☐
Is there conflict?	YES ☐	NO ☐
Are the consequences of this chapter followed up?	YES ☐	NO ☐

CHAPTER THIRTY:

Are the characters described (their current action, appearance, emotions)?	YES ☐	NO ☐
Are more senses than just sight utilised (e.g. taste, smell)?	YES ☐	NO ☐
Does the plot progress?	YES ☐	NO ☐
Are all necessary characters in this chapter?	YES ☐	NO ☐
Is there conflict?	YES ☐	NO ☐
Are the consequences of this chapter followed up?	YES ☐	NO ☐

CHAPTER THIRTY-ONE:

Are the characters described (their current action, appearance, emotions)?	YES ☐	NO ☐
Are more senses than just sight utilised (e.g. taste, smell)?	YES ☐	NO ☐
Does the plot progress?	YES ☐	NO ☐
Are all necessary characters in this chapter?	YES ☐	NO ☐
Is there conflict?	YES ☐	NO ☐
Are the consequences of this chapter followed up?	YES ☐	NO ☐

CHAPTER THIRTY-TWO:

Are the characters described (their current action, appearance, emotions)?   YES ☐   NO ☐

Are more senses than just sight utilised (e.g. taste, smell)?   YES ☐   NO ☐

Does the plot progress?   YES ☐   NO ☐

Are all necessary characters in this chapter?   YES ☐   NO ☐

Is there conflict?   YES ☐   NO ☐

Are the consequences of this chapter followed up?   YES ☐   NO ☐

CHAPTER THIRTY-THREE:

Are the characters described (their current action, appearance, emotions)?   YES ☐   NO ☐

Are more senses than just sight utilised (e.g. taste, smell)?   YES ☐   NO ☐

Does the plot progress?   YES ☐   NO ☐

Are all necessary characters in this chapter?   YES ☐   NO ☐

Is there conflict?   YES ☐   NO ☐

Are the consequences of this chapter followed up?   YES ☐   NO ☐

CHAPTER THIRTY-FOUR:

Are the characters described (their current action, appearance, emotions)?   YES ☐   NO ☐

Are more senses than just sight utilised (e.g. taste, smell)?   YES ☐   NO ☐

Does the plot progress?   YES ☐   NO ☐

Are all necessary characters in this chapter?   YES ☐   NO ☐

Is there conflict?   YES ☐   NO ☐

Are the consequences of this chapter followed up?   YES ☐   NO ☐

CHAPTER THIRTY-FIVE:

Are the characters described (their current action, appearance, emotions)? YES ☐ NO ☐

Are more senses than just sight utilised (e.g. taste, smell)? YES ☐ NO ☐

Does the plot progress? YES ☐ NO ☐

Are all necessary characters in this chapter? YES ☐ NO ☐

Is there conflict? YES ☐ NO ☐

Are the consequences of this chapter followed up? YES ☐ NO ☐

CHAPTER THIRTY-SIX:

Are the characters described (their current action, appearance, emotions)? YES ☐ NO ☐

Are more senses than just sight utilised (e.g. taste, smell)? YES ☐ NO ☐

Does the plot progress? YES ☐ NO ☐

Are all necessary characters in this chapter? YES ☐ NO ☐

Is there conflict? YES ☐ NO ☐

Are the consequences of this chapter followed up? YES ☐ NO ☐

CHAPTER THIRTY-SEVEN:

Are the characters described (their current action, appearance, emotions)? YES ☐ NO ☐

Are more senses than just sight utilised (e.g. taste, smell)? YES ☐ NO ☐

Does the plot progress? YES ☐ NO ☐

Are all necessary characters in this chapter? YES ☐ NO ☐

Is there conflict? YES ☐ NO ☐

Are the consequences of this chapter followed up? YES ☐ NO ☐

CHAPTER THIRTY-EIGHT:

Are the characters described (their current action, appearance, emotions)?   YES ☐ NO ☐

Are more senses than just sight utilised (e.g. taste, smell)?   YES ☐ NO ☐

Does the plot progress?   YES ☐ NO ☐

Are all necessary characters in this chapter?   YES ☐ NO ☐

Is there conflict?   YES ☐ NO ☐

Are the consequences of this chapter followed up?   YES ☐ NO ☐

CHAPTER THIRTY-NINE:

Are the characters described (their current action, appearance, emotions)?   YES ☐ NO ☐

Are more senses than just sight utilised (e.g. taste, smell)?   YES ☐ NO ☐

Does the plot progress?   YES ☐ NO ☐

Are all necessary characters in this chapter?   YES ☐ NO ☐

Is there conflict?   YES ☐ NO ☐

Are the consequences of this chapter followed up?   YES ☐ NO ☐

CHAPTER FORTY:

Are the characters described (their current action, appearance, emotions)?   YES ☐ NO ☐

Are more senses than just sight utilised (e.g. taste, smell)?   YES ☐ NO ☐

Does the plot progress?   YES ☐ NO ☐

Are all necessary characters in this chapter?   YES ☐ NO ☐

Is there conflict?   YES ☐ NO ☐

Are the consequences of this chapter followed up?   YES ☐ NO ☐

CHAPTER FORTY-ONE:

Are the characters described (their current action, appearance, emotions)?	YES ☐	NO ☐
Are more senses than just sight utilised (e.g. taste, smell)?	YES ☐	NO ☐
Does the plot progress?	YES ☐	NO ☐
Are all necessary characters in this chapter?	YES ☐	NO ☐
Is there conflict?	YES ☐	NO ☐
Are the consequences of this chapter followed up?	YES ☐	NO ☐

CHAPTER FORTY-TWO:

Are the characters described (their current action, appearance, emotions)?	YES ☐	NO ☐
Are more senses than just sight utilised (e.g. taste, smell)?	YES ☐	NO ☐
Does the plot progress?	YES ☐	NO ☐
Are all necessary characters in this chapter?	YES ☐	NO ☐
Is there conflict?	YES ☐	NO ☐
Are the consequences of this chapter followed up?	YES ☐	NO ☐

CHAPTER FORTY-THREE:

Are the characters described (their current action, appearance, emotions)?	YES ☐	NO ☐
Are more senses than just sight utilised (e.g. taste, smell)?	YES ☐	NO ☐
Does the plot progress?	YES ☐	NO ☐
Are all necessary characters in this chapter?	YES ☐	NO ☐
Is there conflict?	YES ☐	NO ☐
Are the consequences of this chapter followed up?	YES ☐	NO ☐

CHAPTER FORTY-FOUR:

Are the characters described (their current action, appearance, emotions)? YES [ ] NO [ ]

Are more senses than just sight utilised (e.g. taste, smell)? YES [ ] NO [ ]

Does the plot progress? YES [ ] NO [ ]

Are all necessary characters in this chapter? YES [ ] NO [ ]

Is there conflict? YES [ ] NO [ ]

Are the consequences of this chapter followed up? YES [ ] NO [ ]

CHAPTER FORTY-FIVE:

Are the characters described (their current action, appearance, emotions)? YES [ ] NO [ ]

Are more senses than just sight utilised (e.g. taste, smell)? YES [ ] NO [ ]

Does the plot progress? YES [ ] NO [ ]

Are all necessary characters in this chapter? YES [ ] NO [ ]

Is there conflict? YES [ ] NO [ ]

Are the consequences of this chapter followed up? YES [ ] NO [ ]

CHAPTER FORTY-SIX:

Are the characters described (their current action, appearance, emotions)? YES [ ] NO [ ]

Are more senses than just sight utilised (e.g. taste, smell)? YES [ ] NO [ ]

Does the plot progress? YES [ ] NO [ ]

Are all necessary characters in this chapter? YES [ ] NO [ ]

Is there conflict? YES [ ] NO [ ]

Are the consequences of this chapter followed up? YES [ ] NO [ ]

CHAPTER FORTY-SEVEN:

Are the characters described (their current action, appearance, emotions)? YES ☐ NO ☐

Are more senses than just sight utilised (e.g. taste, smell)? YES ☐ NO ☐

Does the plot progress? YES ☐ NO ☐

Are all necessary characters in this chapter? YES ☐ NO ☐

Is there conflict? YES ☐ NO ☐

Are the consequences of this chapter followed up? YES ☐ NO ☐

CHAPTER FORTY-EIGHT:

Are the characters described (their current action, appearance, emotions)? YES ☐ NO ☐

Are more senses than just sight utilised (e.g. taste, smell)? YES ☐ NO ☐

Does the plot progress? YES ☐ NO ☐

Are all necessary characters in this chapter? YES ☐ NO ☐

Is there conflict? YES ☐ NO ☐

Are the consequences of this chapter followed up? YES ☐ NO ☐

CHAPTER FORTY-NINE:

Are the characters described (their current action, appearance, emotions)? YES ☐ NO ☐

Are more senses than just sight utilised (e.g. taste, smell)? YES ☐ NO ☐

Does the plot progress? YES ☐ NO ☐

Are all necessary characters in this chapter? YES ☐ NO ☐

Is there conflict? YES ☐ NO ☐

Are the consequences of this chapter followed up? YES ☐ NO ☐

CHAPTER FIFTY:

Are the characters described (their current action, appearance, emotions)?	YES ☐	NO ☐
Are more senses than just sight utilised (e.g. taste, smell)?	YES ☐	NO ☐
Does the plot progress?	YES ☐	NO ☐
Are all necessary characters in this chapter?	YES ☐	NO ☐
Is there conflict?	YES ☐	NO ☐
Are the consequences of this chapter followed up?	YES ☐	NO ☐

EPILOGUE:

Are the characters described (their current action, appearance, emotions)?	YES ☐	NO ☐
Are more senses than just sight utilised (e.g. taste, smell)?	YES ☐	NO ☐
Does the plot progress?	YES ☐	NO ☐
Are all necessary characters in this chapter?	YES ☐	NO ☐
Is there conflict?	YES ☐	NO ☐
Are the consequences of this chapter followed up?	YES ☐	NO ☐

The Nitty Gritty

And then, before sending your manuscript off to your editor, have you:

Checked the Loose Ends page of this book

Run a spell-check

Read your novel aloud (or utilised a text-to-voice tool). This is a great way to check for errors.

Looked for over-used words or phrases

Checked for smart or straight quote marks and apostrophes (whichever you've chosen, make sure it's consistent)

Double-checked your timeline is accurate

Confirmed that you've only used exclamation marks when absolutely necessary ☐

Read your manuscript so often that you're sick of it, and you need a break ☐

Tip: *Remember, your editor is the person who can take your very best manuscript to the next level. If you can still improve your novel, it's not yet ready for a professional — you're the best person to push it to that point.*

Promotional Material

The Blurb

Every book must have a blurb—often one of the most-disliked parts of writing for many authors!

Brainstorm your blurb to try and capture what your story is really about and get a head start on enticing your readers.

The Tagline

The tagline or hook is an essential part of a good marketing campaign for your book. This can be used when advertising, or on the front cover of your book.

When creating your tagline, think about the conflict and stakes in your book. Great taglines depict these.

Keep taglines memorable, catchy and at the absolute maximum, two sentences in length. Always make sure they are true to your story. Remember to be punchy and brief, and do not mention the book's title — you don't need to say it twice.

Tip: *Try out your taglines on some of your most trusted readers or friends and family to find the most effective one.*

Key words

Advertising is a very real part of selling your book in today's climate. As you write, certain key words may come to mind that you can use to help promote your title on Amazon or Facebook. Try to think outside just standard genre and go deeper — what makes your book unique?

Use this page to brainstorm some ideas for key words.

Teasers

When the magic happens, it's simply magic! Sometimes, you write a line and you know, you *just know* that it's good. It's so good, you have to use it as a teaser.

Or, perhaps you've had a beta reader highlight that one sentence of dialogue, telling you how much he or she loved it, with exclamation marks, heart symbols and shouty caps for emphasis. This is a great place to keep track of all your book's quotable quotes so when you need one to use for marketing later, it's very easy to find.

Thank You

Thank you so much for purchasing *The Novel Handbook*. I really hope this book assists you in your writing journey.

If you're looking for more tools to help make creating a book easier, visit:

www.laurenclarkeediting.com

and sign up to the mailing list for lots of great ideas. You're also welcome to join our goal-setting Facebook group, where we help you stay on top of your weekly and yearly goals. Visit:

www.facebook.com/groups/numberachievers

Finally, if you enjoyed this book, I would love it if you left it a positive review at your place of purchase.